C A T   E Y E S

D1446676

CAT EYES

true stories of 11 rescued cats

••••••••

CHLOE LANTZY

TATE PUBLISHING & *Enterprises*

Published by Tate Publishing & Enterprises, LLC
127 E. Trade Center Terrace | Mustang, Oklahoma 73064 USA
1.888.361.9473 | www.tatepublishing.com

Tate Publishing is committed to excellence in the publishing industry. The company reflects the philosophy established by the founders, based on Psalm 68:11,
"The Lord gave the word and great was the company of those who published it."

Book design copyright © 2011 by Tate Publishing, LLC. All rights reserved.
Cover design by Kristen Verser
Interior design by April Marciszewski

Published in the United States of America

ISBN: 978-1-61346-360-4
1. Pets: Cats: General
2. Biography & Autobiography: Personal Memoirs
11.08.03

DEDICATION

· · · · · · · ·

This book is dedicated especially to my mother, without whose gentle and patient coaxing these stories would never have moved from my heart to others.

To my father, whose easy love for any and all beings served to support me in my childhood animal pursuits and to open my eyes to their intrinsic nature.

And to Oglethorpe, who entered my life with a solidness of flow so intrinsic to the synchronistic tickings of the divine that somewhere his entrance was surely being applauded.

PROLOGUE

· · · · · · · ·

A stray dog was the first pet our family had. I was, if memory serves me correctly, in second grade. I was, at the least, old enough to be outside after sunset. I can see a miniature version of myself, wrapped snugly in a winter coat, head covered with a cotton babushka so common in the 1950s in our hometown. I can see myself in front of my family home and the streetlights shining onto the main highway that runs past it. Even today, fifty years later, I vividly recall that light shining down through the lattice created by the branches of trees towering overhead.

That is the background of my memory. In the foreground is myself walking along, glancing tenderly backward at a puppy who is following floppily behind.

· · · · · · · ·

My mother tells me that I insisted this pup followed me *accidentally* home, and she laughs at the "accidental" aspect. I believe I didn't coax (much); but under whatever pretense, he arrived that evening; we both agree that he ambled through the back door into our kitchen, ate heartily, settled down for a nap in my lap, and from there, slipped gently into the center of my family's heart.

Oglethorpe, as he was named, was a Heinz 57 version of a mutt, complete with German shepherd markings, though way too small to pass as one. My older brother granted him the title. I don't know where or how he chose that name, nor do I know why I wasn't the one to name the puppy who mysteriously followed *me* home. I suspect it was because my brother had assigned himself the position of name titler and that was accepted without question in our family structure. I am certain that my brother also created songs "of the Og" during the first years we had him, though I can't recall them. I do have memories of him calling Oglethorpe home for the night.

He would sing the three syllables of Oglethorpe's name playfully out into the night, and while we laughed in anticipation, Oglethorpe would magically appear from the shadows eagerly home from whatever pursuits had taken his fancy that particular day.

I have a photo of Oglethorpe where he sits in our kitchen, head down, as he peers unmoving, at our newly acquired Easter chicks and ducklings, all standing peacefully in a row in front of him. Perhaps one of the penetrating qualities of Oglethorpe was his quiet acceptance of whatever was happening around him. He was never trained. In the chaos of a home filled with three children (ages three, seven, and nine) who had their own separate inner growings and outer attentions to deal with, along with a busy attorney father and a community-involved mother, he endured because he asked for so little in return: food, table scraps, and a dish of water. With these small payments, he silently watched over our family. And when we weren't around, he entertained himself about town.

I don't know where he went when he wasn't home with us. Dog catchers were uncommon, and neighborhood dogs came and went as they pleased. Occasionally, they would pack up and join in a

· · · · · · ·

romp through the back alleys, but mostly it seems, they kept to their own doings.

Inner photographs of Ogle flow through my memory's weave like stars in the night's sky, shining out with vibrancy in the midst of time's stillness: there he is, getting a bath, he's bearing it like a man—but once freed, off he flies around and around the yard, rolling and rubbing against the ground. There he is, licking a raw, deep gash on the ankle of a horse. My horse, Sydney (named by my brother), had tangled himself up in a rope and thrashed until he tore through the skin. Og ministered to him until it was healed. And finally, there is Og, weaving about our horses as we head out on a ride through the woods. He always trailed our riding adventures, accompanied often by other dogs we had over the years. Dogs who came and went and surface in my memory just barely as faces and names.

I wonder, when I think of the horse riding days (I was then a teen), how we took for granted that our dogs would follow us in our journeys through the woods. My dogs today, given the same opportunity, would run off. They would reappear at home hours later, panting and full of themselves, but they would certainly not choose to accompany us. Ogle chose to follow us on our horses and not waiver from that self-assigned duty. I wonder if this was an outcome of the lifestyle dogs led back then, where they were completely and absolutely free to come and go as they chose. But it was that same freedom that got him in the end.

A dog warden, or maybe the concept of "pounds," or perhaps a local ordinance, must have finally made it to our town because one day Ogie had his own strange doghouse and was tied to it. Now, for the first time in his ten-plus years of companionship to our family, he protested. He protested and protested and protested and protested. He ran and leaped against his chain and barked nonstop, relentlessly. I don't know how long this scenario played itself out, though it feels like it went on for days. Certainly long enough for him to dig a clear pattern in a circle around the doghouse. I don't know when he would, if ever, have submitted to a chained life because we gave in first—unanimously. The chain was undone, the doghouse abandoned, and Ogle returned to his free reign about town.

· · · · · · · ·

And reign he did for a little while longer, until the hot summer afternoon when the next-door neighbor, my younger brother's friend, came to the same back door through which Oglethorpe had entered as a pup. I have a very shadowy memory of this moment, but it still lies in my heart like the first loss of innocence will. It was announced that Oglethorpe's body, hit by a car, had been found along the main street. I would not believe it until he produced Og's worn, green leather collar. Shortly afterward, my brothers went off to bury him. I didn't go along. I never saw Oglethorpe's furry, loving face again.

I realize now that I took that moment deep inside my heart and placed a piece of it at the bottom of my belly and stashed some other pieces of it behind my eyes because I am feeling those scattered emotional pieces arise from those places inside as I write this—it was a pivotal lesson. In my innocence, and in my egocentric teenage grasp of life, Og's companionship was assumed to be as timeless and as forever as the parents and the home I'd always known. In reality, his gift to us, like a flower's bloom, was ordained to be shared for a brief time only.

Such pristine and bittersweet a memory, this buried sadness over my first real loss suffered that day. The rest of this story, my love for strays, is happening today, I'm positive, because Oglethorpe chose me that soft winter evening of my childhood.

* * * * * * * *

ELEVEN IN ALL

december 30, 2009

It's 7:00 a.m., winter, and the woodstove's died down—I know this because my nose is cold.

Barely moving from my warm space under the blankets, I scout around to see where my company arranged themselves during the night. This particular morning, I can spot Buddy curled at my feet, Silk sleeping in a box under my desk, and Uma asleep on the dresser. But as I shift my position to better view them, the door to my bedroom opens and shuts. My bedroom door is light and doesn't latch, so my cats are able to come and go at will. When one of them comes in, I can't see it; instead, I see the door move as though a ghost is wafting through, and I must wait to be surprised.

This morning's first arrival is Loki, my gangly teen kitten. He slips around under the bed and pops up in front of my face, zooming in for an intimate nose-to-nose. I peer back into his eyes and grin into his haphazardly whiskered face (a by-product of exploring tight spaces). He knows he has my attention and steps back just a step with his left front leg curled up close to his chest. He has always employed this unusual back step, and I find myself waiting for it. After this, he either heads for the cat dish under my vanity where I hear him crunching or chooses to come into the bed and curl up as close to my face as he can fit. This takes some doing because he is really serious about the proximity, and he turns and twirls about while I deal with hair and tail and whiskers until he is settled and begins to purr his soft, cautious Loki purr.

· · · · · · · ·

I'd love to remain in this position, all warm and snuggled in against his purring body, but Loki times this ritual just as I awaken. While he purrs, I check if any other of my cats are located within foot or hand-petting distance. If they are, I rub against them, and stereo purrs begin humming—it's a good way to start the day.

When Uma is sleeping within reaching distance, I touch her soft, silky fur and listen as her purr motor revs up. She has the loudest purr motor of any cat I've ever had, and I never tire of the way it fills the room. This morning though, she's not reachable, but as I lay there listening to Loki and nudging Buddy with my foot to get him to purr (he usually meows in protest instead), I hear Uma fall with a thud off the dresser. She has a tendency to not consider proximity to edges.

My next move is to gently relocate Loki, turn on the light, and pull on my robe while my movements are followed by several sets of cat eyes. They watch me maneuver but generally prefer to get up later. I just pat them on their heads as I go by, and this morning pause to console Uma, who is embarrassed about her fall, though pretending she's fine.

* * * * * * * *

At the bottom of the stairs, I'm greeted by Sonny Sunshine, my orange and white tabby. He mews his odd, tight mew and reaches up against my legs with his paws—and claws—outstretched. If I'm not ready for this display of Sonny's affection, his claws are rude awakeners! But I've learned to be prepared and reach down to pick him up. He sits on my arm like a baby and leans into me, purring and rubbing his face against my shoulder while I turn on the coffee pot and enter the living room, where I attempt to put wood in the woodstove. This takes a bit of juggling because Sonny is a five-year-old cat with a bit of a tummy and he protests my weaving with a tail that begins to flash in consternation. Generally, I give up on doing both at the same time and set Sonny down; he is never okay with that, so I put him down swiftly and back away. I admonish him to settle down. Give him a few minutes, and we're friends again.

As I head back to the kitchen, I give my tortoiseshell, Tippy, sleeping in a chair next to the woodstove, a pat on her little head. I also reach down to pat Murphy, who comes out of somewhere cooler—probably the laundry room—but he shakes me off when he assesses that I'm not producing food yet. I briefly glimpse behind the TV to greet Pinky, who lives (and hides) there throughout the winter. She looks at me, her pink nose quivering, and meows loudly back at my unspoken question: "Everything okay?"

Back in the kitchen and passing the front door, I hear the dogs thundering tumultuously from the porch as they have heard me and are, as always, antsy to come in and greet me. I open the door to their joyful morning exuberance and watch Mister Hobbs, his tabby tail high, slip in behind them, while Loki zips out full of the zestful innocence of a youth who doesn't understand the chill of ten degrees Fahrenheit.

Prince, my white fire Siamese, has yet to surface, but I know he's around, just tucked away since he elected not to sleep with me last night; I know he'll sneak up during the day to have the bed all to himself. Io, my oldest cat of thirteen years, greets me from the kitchen chair where she spends most of her time, and I make sure to give her a moment of cuddly attention before I finally pour my morning's coffee.

There. I've introduced all eleven of the cats who are sharing this winter of 2009 with me. You may label me a crazy cat woman, but be aware that I didn't plan it this way.

The truth is that there is a crisis of severe overpopulation in the cat world, and my eleven rescues are not even cleaning up a drop in the ocean of suffering endured daily right in our neighborhoods and often in our own backyards. I think many people consider cats to be semiwild animals, capable of fending for themselves and lacking worth, much less feelings or personality. I hope that by telling their stories, you won't fall for that line of rationale next time you discover a homeless cat peering at you from the bushes.

As my favorite storybook character, Horton the elephant, says: "A person's a person, no matter how small." In the chapters that follow, I would like to introduce you to these small, furry "persons" who floated in on specks of dust and yelled, "Yopp" into my heart.

· · · · · · · ·

SONNY SUNSHINE

the problem child

Sonny Sunshine was the most bedraggled cat I'd ever met. His fur was matted with cow manure, his breathing congested, he drooled from a mouth that held only half its teeth, and his breath stank.

But he leaned against my legs and begged to be held in my arms, where he nestled and rubbed his head against my shoulder with feline persistence, purring as though we were best friends. I asked the farmer if I could have Sonny and, gaining permission along with a quizzical rise of his eyebrows, Sonny came home with me that day.

I don't normally intuit a cat's name right away, but on our short ride home, I clearly understood that his name was Sonny Sunshine. I thought this was pretty funny since he looked more like "Cloudy Rainstorm," but I didn't argue the point.

At home, Sonny settled in as though inside living was something he knew how to do, and he began seriously cleaning himself up. Daily he washed his orange and white coat for hours until he was soaked in a saliva bath. After several days of this, I began to worry that this was a peculiar neurosis, but he stopped as soon as he had completely washed away the cow manure scent. I guess he didn't like it any more than I did. I discovered that he was already neutered, so his history prior to his years at the barn was a "drop off," meaning he originally had a home, but his family dropped him off where they assumed he could live. "After all, he's a cat" is not an uncommon rationale.

Sonny apparently didn't do well making the transition to the barn life where he lived for several years before he found me. The farmer told me the regular barn cats took advantage of his housecat ways. They wouldn't leave him near the proffered food that was left out for them. Perhaps his rotted teeth were the reason he was dropped off, but I'd guess he acquired that from years of nutritional deficiency. The vet told me he had "lung worms" and that this was unusual.

"Cats get these kinds of worms from eating snails," he said. So that was how Sonny kept himself alive, eating snails. Yuck. I've never seen him indulge in snails since he's moved in with us— apparently, not his meal of choice.

Sonny soon had the rest of his teeth removed, which cleared up his bad breath, drooling, and runny nose. He eats now by simply swallowing his food, but I wonder how long he had to deal with that and how painful it must have been for him to eat or breathe; yet still, he approached me that day, a stranger, asking to be held and purred hopefully in my arms.

This was the summer of 2008, and my position as a cat advocate had been growing for some time. I had already placed a dozen or so stray pets into good homes and considered my four-acre country home "topped out" for owning homeless cats with a grand total of seven. I welcomed him in figuring that I'd find him a good home once he was a healthy cat, but I discovered there was a glitch to that plan.

Sonny has two white markings down his cheeks from the corners of his eyes that look quite similar to war paint on a person's face. I'm mentioning this because he lived up to his war paint look the day after he decided he was clean of the barn smells and jumped down from his perch. I watched him as he approached one of my sleeping cats, and to her surprise (and mine), slapped her across the face with his open claws. This was only the beginning. Sonny worked his way through my entire cat population with his wild lightning attacks and, despite strongly hollered reprimands, he stalked and struck until all knew Sonny wasn't going to take any guff from any of them. Not that they were out for guff—they were peaceful cats—but I couldn't tell that to Sonny!

Noting this quirk of his, I decided I would need to find him a home where he would be the only cat, but that plan soon changed too. I discovered another glitch in his character. Sonny would often slip into my lap and stretch out there purring happily. Then inexplicably, his attitude would change, and he would turn on me too with his lightning clawed attacks. After being startled by this a few times, I learned to watch for the shift by keeping an eye on his tail. It would begin to twitch in an increasingly stiff manner, slashing back and forth just prior to the attack, followed by a leap away, a stiffed-legged strut, and a display of vicious scratching at the nearest piece of furniture. Well, this aspect of his character certainly wasn't going to land him a home!

I have concluded that Sonny suffers from post-traumatic stress disorder. He can only handle so much intimacy, then something strikes a deeper chord—the memory that he has been abandoned with the immediate result: he gets angry, fearful, and insecure and acts out. Sonny wasn't going to find a home with that kind of reactive behavior. I certainly wasn't about to return him to the barn or send him off to the local shelter, where he didn't stand a chance of surviving. So what could I do but keep him?

But this is not a curse—don't get me wrong. I'm blessed, I feel, with the opportunity to rescue such a long-suffering cat, and over the two years I've had him, I've watched his angry and sudden fits decrease dramatically. He no longer strikes out at me and has even made a cautious cat friend or two (Loki and Hobbs). These days, he monitors his own stress levels and leaps away from me when he's reached maximum trust capacity.

I've also noticed that each fall season, Sonny gets a little more nerved up than during the rest of the year. I think some part of him remembers the time when he found himself alone in a cold world filled with cows and territorial barn cats. I theorize that that memory haunts him and that it becomes triggered by the seasonal shift.

I've shared my life with enough pets to see that they don't release the memory of their individual traumas as easily as we'd like to believe. Like people, some are better about letting go than others. Sonny perhaps had too much time with too much suffering to absolutely trust that he now has a forever home; and in truth, I don't believe his inner terror could handle another sense of abandonment. So meet Sonny Sunshine, the eighth addition to my eleven-member cat family. He's a keeper. He's my Sunshine!

U M A

(dah puma)

Uma is my favorite cat of them all, but I only
whisper that into her attentive ears when none

. . . .

of the others can hear. She is the essence of volup-
tuousness with her long silken white fur and owl-
sized bright eyes, and then there is her personality.
Well, let me go back a bit.

When Uma spotted me, I was walking through
the holding room at the shelter, where a year earlier, I
had accepted a position as its business manager. The
holding room was a room where animals recovering
from illnesses were kept and incoming cats awaited
their life or death determination. The honest truth
is that there are so many cats brought in to this rural
shelter that only two out of every ten actually make
it out to the adoption room. Please be aware of this
next time you choose to take the stray kittens or cats
that show up in your backyard to your local shelter.
Cats have virtually no legal rights and are frequently
being euthanized even as you drive out of the park-
ing lot. This is the honest and painful truth.

I had learned to avoid connecting with the cats
being held in the holding room because it was too
heart wrenching to guess their fate. Yet I had to
walk through this room in order to access the rest
of the building, so on this day in the early fall of
2006, I happened to walk by Uma's crate. I wasn't

looking in her direction, but there was a loud *thunk,* and I glanced over. I saw Uma sitting up on her back feet, having plunked her forelegs down on the bars. She was looking intensely at me with her large owl eyes as if to say, "Hey, you there, like, what am I doing here?"

I drifted over, despite myself, to check out this unexpected communication and recognized that she wasn't going to make the cut. According to the basic criteria for adoptable cats, health was one of the first factors taken into consideration. Uma was bone thin with matted fur, had discharge from her eyes and nose, and remnants of diarrhea stained her fur. I shook my head sadly and walked away. At home, I now owned six cats and was determined to be practical; after all, this was a shelter, and I certainly (I told myself) couldn't take home every cat that couldn't be adopted.

But the next day, I couldn't resist looking for her, and she was *still* there and still looking at me with those beautiful intelligent eyes of hers. I knew in my heart that I couldn't walk away this time. Not this time. Not this one. So much for practical.

When Uma arrived home with me, my husband asked, eyebrows raised, if this was another cat that I was going to place elsewhere, and I had to reply in all honesty and not without an inner pang of guilt, "I don't know." Even then, I guessed it was too late, there was something about Uma that had already embedded itself into my heart.

Upon research, I found that her unusual markings—golden spots on top of her head and golden saddlebag markings on her shoulders, silken soft fur, a pressed-in nose and big round eyes—indicated genetics from that of the feline purebred called a Turkish van. The description I read starts out: "This large, intelligent cat…" and goes on to say that they were a breed isolated to Turkey until 1987 when they began appearing in the United States. Somehow, just eighteen years ago, Uma's bloodline had made its way to the small rural area of Bradford County, Pennsylvania.

Uma took some time to physically recover from what was caused, I'm sure, from a nutritionally deficient kittenhood. I tried to contact the woman who had brought her in, but her phone was disconnected. I'm guessing that Uma was just another young cat from some neighborhood cat's litter and that the people who had been feeding her were moving away so she was taken to the shelter. The vet said that her diarrhea, which didn't respond to wormer or antibiotic treatments, was indicative of a food allergy and that she would need to eat specific foods for the rest of her life. I didn't intuitively believe this diagnosis. I felt that Uma's problem was an intestinal tract that needed time to recover from a prolonged deficiency in her diet, so I instead fed her food designated for a sensitive stomach; over six month's time, her diarrhea lessened, and she was eventually able to eat the same food, as the rest of my cats with no ill effects.

She still does get diarrhea occasionally but only from beef and, intriguingly, she self-regulates this by refusing to eat any beef products. Even in canned cat food, a favorite treat, she will smell the beef and back away with a grimace while my other cats glutton themselves. When she does happen to have a diarrhea reaction to something—rarely anymore—she is highly embarrassed when it clings to her long fur. She allows me at such moments to wash her off in the laundry room sink. She protests loudly and indignantly but doesn't fight me, and she certainly could.

After she had the chance to heal up from the skinny, besotted kitten she was initially, I had several friends, upon meeting Uma, offer to adopt her right there on the spot. This never happens! But I was smitten too, and their offers were declined. I only had four cats at the time, making Uma a mere fifth cat. Five cats are a stretch, but doable, I decided.

So what is so special about Uma? She's breathtakingly gorgeous, but many cats are. Her real specialness is in her high level of almost human intelligence, purity of selfhood, and her particularly interactive personality. She holds some kind of innate regal stance that runs through to her core and upwells from her inner being. In fact, her response to life has become an ongoing lesson to me as a human. If I could only attain her absolute purity of intent and her guilelessness in self-expression that is so inherent to her nature. Uma is never for a moment out of synch—she just is.

I am at a loss for words for sharing Uma's unique persona. But I'll try by describing a few of her ways;

however, her ways are complex and ever changing even now, three years into knowing her.

When anyone shows up at my house to visit, it won't be long before Uma abruptly appears and plops down in the person's lap, purring as though she's known him all her life. She flirts intensely, and generally everyone but the most adamant cat-evaders dutifully complies to her expectations of responsive stroking. She does have her favorite visitors though, and for them, she reserves her special feline flirtations. This may include a well-placed and serious swipe of her open-clawed paw if they pass her by. For all her delicious beauty, she is a demanding lady.

When she first arrived and was recuperating, she took over a comfy basket set up by the window. My other cats, surprisingly, left her alone there. So it was notable, some months later, to see our big gentle cat, Buddy, sleeping in Uma's basket with her casually relaxing near by. After this, Uma befriended the male cats and ignored or stalked the females—a trend she continues to this day.

When I'm making the bed, Uma will insist on sitting in the middle of it while I continue making it by arranging the sheets and covers on top of her.

She is mesmerized by this experience, and I love watching as her form beneath the covers finds its leisurely way out. If any box or container is put anywhere in the house, it won't be long before Uma is sitting on top of, or inside of, the container. She is mystified by new kinesthetic experiences, and the exploration of any new solid object gives her remarkable pleasure. I have occasionally found her turned upside down, batlike, hanging off the edge of a chair seat. I don't know whether it's the kinesthetic experience or the unique perspective that this stance provides, but she seems to be deep in thought when I've spotted her like this.

She disapproves of the group water bowl (it's cleaned every day, but that doesn't matter); she prefers to drink at the faucet in the bathroom usually when I am trying to brush my teeth. Guess who wins out for first dibs to the running water?

Uma also disapproves of that dirty stuff of messing with mice or moles. She is distinctly a cat bred for higher fare; however, this summer, she surprised me. I was outside at the picnic table when I heard a rustling in the nearby flower garden, then Uma appeared and dropped a mouse in front of me. Actually, she didn't drop it, she spat it out alive and looked at me as if to say, "Ugh, what *is* so great about this?" I immediately took Uma inside, expecting her to fight me (the rest of my cats would fight hard to return to their prey), but Uma had already forgotten about it. It was obvious she had no intention of returning to the scene of that messy crime.

Shortly after the distasteful mouse episode, Uma began stalking butterflies. We have a garden of milkweed specifically planted to assist monarch butterflies, and Uma figured out that this provided a bounty of great fun floating through the air. She began sitting next to the milkweed garden, and it wasn't long before we found mangled butterflies everywhere. Needless to say, this couldn't stand, and we were forced to admonish our regal Uma when she approached the milkweed garden. Thankfully, it didn't take long before she gave up her game. If she could talk, she would probably say that she was getting bored anyway.

Other than her intense purr, she's a quiet cat, but should anyone attempt to get cheese (her favorite snack) out of the refrigerator, Uma's going to make more noise than a pack of coyotes on a hot scent. She will squeak and squawk, stretch up, full-bodied against the counter, her head jerking in every direction, appearing to be absolutely losing her mind. She'll swat vigorously at the food being proffered, and sometimes, annoyingly, knock it out of the dish I'm setting down. My other cats, recognizing her battle cry, know to come in for a treat too, but they wait patiently nearby. Distinct difference.

My son says that Uma gets away with much more than the other cats just because she is so gorgeous; he has a point, but I think she would get away with all that she does even if she weren't visually perfect. She's just Uma—the special one. I'm so glad that on that day at the shelter, she insisted on receiving an answer to her question. Indeed, *whatever was* she doing on death's row?

· · · · · · ·

38

PRINCE, BUDDY, AND TIPPY

"three little kittens ..."

I have three cats that think I am their mother, and though they weren't born here, know no other home than mine. Let me explain.

I was volunteering at the local shelter the summer of 2005 and happened to be there one sweltering Friday afternoon when I saw this scene through the window of the adoption office: a woman crying, a young boy (nine years old maybe) standing quiet and stunned, and a cardboard box. The staff was talking to the woman who was leaving as I came in to sign out for the day. Curious, I peered into the box, afraid to see a dead or wounded cat there; but to my inner relief, there were three living kittens, their eyes still shut. The staff, however, looked pained; they had been antsy to close up and head out for a swim, now this. One informed me that the mother cat had been killed by a car and the woman, not knowing what else to do, brought in the kittens. She was not the owner of the dead cat; it was *just another* neighborhood stray. The problem was that the kittens would require bottle-feeding and could not possibly make it through the night, much less the weekend, at the shelter. The kittens were already notably dehydrated, and the smallest was limp. I waited to see how they would resolve this dilemma, but no one came to the rescue. The staff planned to euthanize them before they left for the day.

You can guess what happened. I drove home with the box and some brief directions on how to care for them. I was told that not only must I bottle-feed them every five hours until they could make it through the night but I would also need to rub their bellies each time in order to help them move their bowels. Apparently, the mother cat does this when she licks their bellies.

That night, I dutifully set my alarm and every five hours got up to warm up their potion of kitten milk. I would bottle-feed each one and then rub each small belly with a warmed-up, wet rag. I was most concerned about the wee one, and apparently so were the staff because they called me the next day to see how the kittens were making out, and I heard an audible sigh when I replied they were *all* alive and well.

Thus began the raising of the troop I fondly titled "the triplets." I kept them in a box by my bed and placed a heating pad under a blanket set on low. They seemed very satisfied with this option, as I would always find them curled up in a threesome ball over the heating pad. When they were able to make it through the night without my involvement, I placed them and their pad, in a large, wire cage, next to a floor-to-ceiling window so they could sense the day and night rhythms. The cage was mainly to keep my dogs and cats away from them, though my cats weren't interested once they saw it was "only kittens." The dogs were more curious. I had three at the time and was impressed to watch Nubi, my mixed golden retriever/basset hound (yes, he is a funny sight), take charge.

Nubi stationed himself next to the kittens almost 24/7 to stand guard. When any other of my pets, especially my other dogs—his best buddies any other time—approached the pen, Nubi would growl fiercely at them. He wasn't pretending either, and they would back away.

Eventually, the kittens opened their eyes and began to explore their world. This is a very fun time for anybody who has had this experience. They toddle and fall, crouch and leap at each other, fall again in a fur-kicking bunch and attempt, falling some more, to climb and play about. It's great entertainment. I would set them out on the couch each day after feeding and let them flail about with Nubi standing guard at my feet.

Their personalities were becoming apparent too. Buddy was a huge orange-colored kitten with comical spots on his nose; he dominated the other two by at least double the size. When I would attempt to bottle-feed him, he would try to get his mouth around the rubber nipple, have great difficulty adjusting, get frustrated, protest, and angrily attack the nipple. It would take some time and patience, but eventually, he would manage to get down his meals this way; however, he never got used to the rubber nipple and knew something wasn't right. Right up until he was weaned, he protested. When he began to have teeth, he would chew in frustrated ire at the proffered nipple and eventually rip it off. It was a fight to the finish every time. I decided the weaning of the triplets was completed the day Buddy ripped off the last nipple on the last bottle I had. I titled him Scrapper Red at that time, but as an adult, he's grown into such a massive, twenty-two-pound, yet easygoing guy, that he's been re-dubbed Mister Buddy.

Meanwhile, Prince, the white kitten with flame point Siamese markings and crystal blue eyes, impressed us with his high IQ. I had attached plastic siding along the sides of their enclosure in order to keep them from crawling out. The siding was attached to the bars and reached up past their ability to climb over, and this worked nicely, as I could keep food, and water, toys and baskets inside with plenty of room for them to romp. Prince, however, got bored with this and set his mind to overcome the barricade. One morning, I found him outside their crate. I wondered how he managed that and set him back in. The next day, there he was again, outside, and I still couldn't figure out how he managed to escape. The third morning, he sat atop the crate, looking as proud as punch, and if a cat can swell his chest in pride, Prince was doing it. Even though the other kittens were fine with their enclosure and had never even thought about escaping, I determined it was the end of the cage phase and set them free.

Last, but certainly not least, was Tippy, a tortoiseshell and the wee one of the three. She received the title of Tippy because her favorite perch (to this day) was on my shoulder. She would, whenever possible, crawl up there where she would sit, wrapped around my neck and viewing the world, perfectly content, from my shoulder. It didn't matter if I was walking; there she would sit, tipping precariously forward and backward (she taught me to hold her tail for stability) yet purring contentedly. When she was older, she began to climb to the top of one of our outbuildings each dusk, and we would see her sitting at the very tippy-top of the roof, watching the sunset. We thought this was romantic until we found out that she was particularly interested in stalking the bats that came out at that time of day. The rooftop was a great vantage point.

She has always been the loner cat, and I've been told by many who deal with different cat types that tortoiseshells tend to be aloof and individualized, for the most part. They aren't known to be big on laps and such cuddling concepts, and I can vouch that the tortoiseshells I've known are like that. As an adult, Tippy has chosen to live outside under one of our outbuildings; she comes inside to hang with the rest of us only during the cold months of the year and, even then, spends nicer winter days outside.

* * * * * * * *

But back to the day I brought the kittens home. They were technically shelter-owned cats, and I had every intention of taking them back, once weaned, to be put up for adoption. I had three cats and three dogs at this time and had promised my husband that that was enough.

But I didn't protest my husband's overt pleasure when the kittens, now freed from their crate, cavorted all about the house and produced, as all youthful pets do, a warm, silly, sometimes messy, but heartfelt atmosphere throughout the downstairs. So when he murmured spontaneously, and no doubt surprised at what was coming out of his mouth, that, what the heck, we might as well keep them, well, I was off to sign the adoption papers before he could renege on that impulse. He had said it out loud and in my presence. Such are the consequences.

Truthfully, if I ever were in a position to take in a group of cats, I would eagerly swell the ranks by adopting a pregnant cat and keeping her and all of her kittens. It is the most pleasurable experience to have a group of cats under one roof that will never hiss or spit at each other and are often sighted sleeping together or grooming each other throughout their lifetime. I suggest that anyone who reads this story and is excited about starting their own cat family search around for a homeless pregnant cat (ask a shelter to contact you when one is brought in) and take her in. You will be delighted, I guarantee it, at both the experience and then the memories that will last a lifetime. Well worth the initial vetting fees.

Today, my baby triplets have grown into a close-knit troop of easy-going cats who take this place for granted because it has been, from the time they opened their eyes to the world, their only home. Nubi has become their unofficial best buddy of the "canine branch." I catch them rubbing against his chest, purring, their tails up and getting in his face, and he appears to be annoyed with these frivolous feline displays of affection—secretly though, I know he wouldn't have it any other way. Me neither.

MISTER
HOBBS

the bachelor cat

M ister Hobbs found me by stumbling out in
front of my car, in my driveway, as I was on
my way to attend a board meeting at the shelter.
As I watched from my car, he collapsed and lay
still. When I immediately checked him over, he

appeared severely emaciated but without any other signs of injury. I didn't take him to the shelter, as I knew by this time what would be his fate in his condition. Instead, I took him to our stable, settled him with a cat bed and a can of wet food, dry food, and water. My rescue mode at that time (spring of 2005) was to offer food and assistance to any pet that wandered into my world but to give them the opportunity to leave, if they chose.

The next day, there was Hobbs basking in the sun nearby so he had decided to remain. I felt an unexpected pleasure that he'd chosen to stay. Perhaps there was an inner knowing that he really needed me, even though I thought his problem was simply lack of food. I only had two cats of my own at the time, Io and Pinky, so an addition to the family was not a concern.

I set up a vet appointment for the following week, but after several days of feeding him, I petted him one day and felt wetness on my hand. I checked it out and found pus coming from his side. I applied some ointment to this, thinking that it was a wound that was now healing. The next day, there was more pus coming from another area, and the day after that, more pus from yet another area. I also noticed when he walked that he was hobbling (thus, his name) on three legs and that his right front leg was stiff. His appetite was strong, and he wasn't in pain, so I wasn't all that worried. I just kept a watch on the pus areas that kept appearing each day and applied ointment. There were about six of these pus areas and all were from his right side.

However by the time I got him into the vet's office, Hobbs was so weak that I carried him in on a basket. The vet did the usual vetting overview and prescribed antibiotics for the pus, which indicated infection. He said that his upper leg was broken, but unless I wanted to get it reset via a trip to a specialist out of state, it should most likely heal on its own. Since Hobbs was in no pain, I elected to let nature take its course.

Throughout that summer, most of the time, Mister Hobbs preferred to lie in his bed in the stable, getting out only to eat and use the litter box. If it were sunny, I would see him relaxing in the sun. He seemed to have no interest in approaching us at the house. The pus areas eventually cleared up, but Hobbs remained weak and, despite his appetite and weight gain, was still not moving much.

I took him in to the vet for a re-check, and this is when I was informed that Hobbs was ill enough that if he didn't respond to a second round of antibiotics, I would probably need to put him to sleep. The vet was concerned that the infection had penetrated deep into his bones. This information was couched in very gentle terms, which I appreciated, but I wasn't going for that option.

I replied, "Well, guess we'll have to pray then." I had gotten to know Hobbs by this time, and I believed in the strength of his desire to live. He just seemed to have that kind of strong internal intention.

And my feelings proved right because Hobbs is still with us. He's become a big husky, brown and black tabby cat, a tiger, but that's not the end of his story.

His was not a simple recovery period. It took him an entire year—from spring of 2005 when I found him until the spring of 2006 before he did more than get out of his basket to eat and bask in the sun. In the fall of 2005, I brought him inside to live in our laundry room, where he could be next to the litter boxes. At this point, the triplets were old enough to roam, and to be sure they would use the litter boxes, they were also spending nights in the laundry room. This setup worked wonderfully. Hobbs was entertained with three bubbly kittens who shared the room with him each night and who, kitten style, would involve him in their antics. He would sniff them and allow them to sleep and frolic around him, and they all remain friends to this day. I was a little concerned come spring when he began to show an increasingly pointed interest in Tippy, the female, but at that point, Hobbs was well enough to undergo surgery so he was neutered.

Watching Hobbs all these years has given me some insights into who he was before he collapsed in my driveway. I live surrounded by fields, woods, and dairy farms, and I believe that Hobbs was originally a feral barn cat, possibly one from generations of barn cats. Even after a year of being indoors with us, once fully recovered, he chose to live outside in the woodshed next to the house. It's taken him years to stop hiding from strangers and other than his recovery winter spent inside, he will only return inside warily, when the temperature sinks below ten degrees.

It took him four years, but he's learned to appreciate the finer elements of sharing space with humans. Right now, as I type this, he is basking in the kitchen window, so relaxed, his tongue is hanging out. His broken upper leg has healed as much as it ever will. He'll always use his three legs more than his fourth, but he can put weight on it. He's in no pain.

Still, Hobbs never jumps in my lap, and he never comes near to request a petting like the others, though I can get him to purr by scratching behind his ears for a while and whispering love messages into his furry, fat head. He's become a grand old guy who romps with the males and chases our lady cats, all in fun. He may be neutered, but he hasn't forgotten that world that he came from! In fact, he's been spotted occasionally in the company of strange feline females. Last summer, I heard such a racket in the woodshed that I had to explore. I climbed up the ladder to get to his area and was calling to him, afraid from the sounds being emitted that he was in severe pain. When I got close to the back of the shed, there was one more intense screech, then Mister Hobbs just so very calmly appeared, sat down at a distance from me, and started to clean himself as if to say "See, lady, it's all fine; you can just move along." I moved along with a grin. I never did see his lady friend; guess she left when she didn't get what Hobbs had promised. Perhaps that's what she was screeching about!

One summer (three years after Hobbs joined us), I brought home a stray, unspayed female who stayed with us until I could place her. Like Hobbs, she had also appeared in the road in front of me (I spotted her in my headlights one rainy night, nursing her one surviving kitten), but that's another story. She was shy around the other cats, but I noticed that she found her way to Hobbs and would hang out with him during the day. I know he helped her adjust while she was waiting for her new home, and I appreciate that.

I've often considered what happened to Hobbs, given his injuries, and I can only come to one conclusion. Hobbs was wounded with a shotgun. Thus, his wounds were scattered, and the blast had enough power to break his leg. I can envision him being a reasonably content feral cat, sleeping out-side in the sun one early spring day when a hunter spots him and, "for the fun of it," sights in on him. If Hobbs hadn't been tough enough to keep going until he found his way to my home, he would've died an excruciating death. In fact, considering his emaciated state, he had already suffered horribly. I'm guessing that it was only because he knew he was dying that he chose to show himself and to take the chance of trusting a human. It's truly a shame that so many people seeing a stray at their doorstep choose to chase them away, not recognizing that often as not, their appearance is an act of despera-tion, a serious SOS for help.

I equate rescuing cats to working in a mash during a war. Here they come, those affected by it: the abandoned, starved, and wounded. There's so many that my personal effort is minute—yet intensely significant to those who suffer under its indiscriminant brutality.

I O

moon child of jupiter

Io is my elder cat and the only one who was actually born here, but to tell her story, I have to introduce you to her mother, Jupiter.

. . . .

Jupiter was a six-month-old black-and-white kitten when she showed up looking in the window of our front door one chilly winter night in 1995. I had two cats at that time, so taking her in was not even a decision. She was welcomed with open arms. And in she came, impressing us at the way she gave our home a once-over, agreed to use the litter box, and, having approved of us, settled in for the winter.

At this point in time, my cats, History and Bonzi (who appeared one morning crawling out of a box that had been dropped in my backyard), had given my dogs dominion of the floor spaces for some reason not understood by me and lived virtually on top of our furniture; but Jupiter's take-charge attitude changed this entire cat-versus-dog game. Shortly after her arrival, without giving it a second thought, she stretched out in feline-sprawled comfort on the living room rug. When the dogs objected to this breaking of the ground rules, they learned all about feline teeth and claws at work, and back she would return to her comfort on the rug as though nothing had happened. Perhaps that strength of personality was what got her to our house healthy and alive from whatever past she came from. She had the toughest, in-charge cat attitude for a mere kitten I'd ever seen.

We soon found out that that past had also brought her to us pregnant, so that winter, she gave birth to three calico kittens whom we named after Jupiter's moons: Io, Gannymead, and Callisto.

Jupiter proved to be the most intensely protective cat to her kittens of any mother cat I've witnessed before or since. She never left their side from the time they were born until they were weaned, and even then, she was always in the same room with them. Other mother cats will stay that close for the first days after birth and then begin to leave for increasingly longer periods of time but not Jupiter.

Today, I wish I had been more informed of what this was telling me about Jupiter. At that time, I didn't have a clue. Any mother cats I'd had prior to this didn't seem to pay much attention when their kittens left them to go to new homes. So once they were weaned, I put out the word and found a home for Ganymede and Callisto, and they went off to their new home as a pair. I was pleased I'd found them a home together, but to my surprise and dismay, Jupiter never got over that loss. She looked and looked for them, then finally reacted by becoming obsessively protective of Io and holding a grudge against our other cats.

Until that point, "Juppy" had ignored History and Bonzi, and they ignored her. Now, she was vengeful. She began to teach Io to stalk and attack them in tandem with her. Jupiter was, as stated, a fierce adversary on her own; but with Io in tow, they were a continual source of stress and anxiety for the others. That spring, Bonzi began living in my closets, and History started hiding outside. By summer, Jupiter and Io were standing guard over the cat dishes and chasing them away if they came near. Jupiter also began eating as much as she could stomach in order to keep them from the food and was getting fat while my other cats were losing weight steadily. I knew I had to do something so I put an ad in the paper for a home for Jupiter, asking for one with no other cats. Since Jupiter was fixed and up to date on her shots, I got a quick response, and she was taken to a loving home shortly after. I did get several updates on her well-being, and she did settle in after a week of hiding under a bed. That sounds unlike her, but I realize in hindsight that her emotions were more complex than most.

Now, we arrive at Io's story, which is a sad but simple one. Io was bereft at the loss of her mother, who had become her best friend in the brief five months of her lifetime. She sulked for a month or two and then befriended my beagle, Berkanna, who had lost her dog buddy about the time Jupiter was rehomed. The two of them were often seen walking down the road side-by-side. Io is a big cat, so they were almost the same size, and it was quite the sight. This worked until we took in another dog (Nubi) and our beagle bonded with him leaving Io to her lonesome. And she was lonesome. She refused, after this loss, to befriend any other pet who has entered this household, and there have been a lot over the thirteen years she's shared with us. She has spent her lifetime with us, always close by but remote inside herself.

In the past couple years, she has laid claim to a chair in our kitchen and sleeps there continually. She hisses at any cat who makes overtures to meet her, so they keep their distance. It's a notable moment when she occasionally allows any cat to touch noses with her. Good news: she has recently begun to just slightly, in an offhand way, befriend our new addition, Murphy.

Since going from the kitchen to the laundry room to use the litter box has become an anxiety-producing journey for her—as she feels she must make her way by hissing and snarling at any cat who looks in her direction—I've established litter privileges in the cellar for her use only. She knows to stand by the cellar door when she needs to use the box, runs down the stairs, and then meows to return. In the summer, she uses the cellar window to access the outdoors. Sometimes, I will see her sitting outside but near the window, enjoying the weather.

She's not beyond some fun and folic though—it's just rare. Once in a while, I'll see her playing around the kitchen, usually after dark when she must feel she's not so visible. Once in a while, too, she'll approach me for some lap sitting. She does this in a dainty, sensitive fashion for such a large-sized and generally unsocial cat. I'll see her sitting in the doorway to the living room from where I'm sitting watching TV, imploring me with her lovely eyes to be invited in for a petting. I call to her, and she comes into my lap but just for a brief time. Once she's had her fill, usually within five to ten minutes, she curtly jumps down and walks back to her bed on the kitchen chair. I've never gotten her to purr.

I suppose the moral of Io's story is that those of us who share our lives with cats need to recognize that while most cats adapt readily to change and loss, not all do. It's important to pay attention to the signs they give us in order to know if their unique personalities can handle the environment we provide and, whenever possible, do what we can to assist them in adjusting when things change. Had I known this, I might have found Io and Jupiter a home together as a pair or kept the entire family of Jupiter's moon kittens. Bottom line, if we aren't watchful, some, like Io, may wind up suffering lifelong depression. I understand this now and am grateful to Jupiter for the lesson she brought home to me by coming into my life thirteen winters ago.

63

SILK

smooth as ...

Silk was an accident that unraveled over time, more than a plan. She arrived in my home as a "foster cat" with four kittens in tow. One of the kennel staff, Deb, had approached me and asked if I would foster her. I imagine Deb had taken a liking to Silk and knew that if she didn't get fostered, she and her kittens would be euthanized. It was late August, the middle of what cat rescue workers call "the kitten season," and 80 percent of the cats or kittens arriving at the shelter were bound to be culled. Needless to say, I didn't question Deb's motives for bringing her to my attention; I agreed to offer to foster her and was given permission to take her and her litter home that day. My intention was to raise the kittens until they were weaned and then return the entire family to the shelter to be adopted. But as I got to know Silk, I recognized that she was not adoption material.

Silk was young and no doubt a first-time mother. She tended to her basic responsibilities for her litter, feeding and cleaning them but when done removed herself from them, choosing to just sit and look out the window. There I would see her throughout each day, sitting quietly, with an air of resignation. She was not fearful but neither was she friendly; she was remote and, to my mind, depressed. Was she sent away to the shelter because she had an unwanted litter? Did she deeply miss her original home? She appeared healthy enough to have been fed and cared for before she was brought to my attention.

After her kittens were weaned at seven weeks, I returned them to the shelter knowing they would be adopted (and they were), but I adopted Silk. Had she stayed at the shelter, due to her remoteness, I knew she would have languished in her small pen, eyeing potential adopters with distant suspicion. Her chances of finding a home, without any knack for showing off were slim to none. Even if she made it out to the adoption room, I guessed it would be just a matter of time before she would be considered unadoptable and euthanized.

My new plan for Silk was to get her spayed and immunized, then seek out a home for her. Silk seemed content enough when I dropped her off in her new in-house environment with a newly married couple who were thrilled to have their first cat; but six months later, I received a call that she wasn't working out. She remained, as I'd feared, remote, and they really wanted a cuddly lap cat. I always guarantee that I will take my rescued cats back if they don't work out for any reason, so Silk came back to me again while I continued to search for an appropriate home.

Silk settled back into my home as though she'd never left. She returned to her perch sitting and staring out the bedroom window and then disappearing into some secluded hideaway where she would sleep and ponder. I say, "ponder" because we decided that Silk was highly intelligent and analytical. We could see it in her deep, quiet eyes and in the set of her jaw. Silk is a pretty black-and-white cat, but unlike most cats, her jaw is distinctly square and juts out—that, coupled with black markings that mask her eyes—gives her a pensive and unique feline look. Given her jawline and her regal personality, she may have some pure blood in her genetics; though to date, we haven't figured out what that might be.

One notable characteristic of Silk is her propensity to sit in boxes. We happened to have had a very small box sitting out at the bottom of the second-story stair steps, and Silk, who to that point had never shown any interest in coming downstairs, was discovered one day sitting inside it. It was so small that she had to sit straight up, but there she sat for the longest time, looking regal and on top of things, as though she figured she was invisible inside that teeny box. We elected to leave it out for her, and when she wanted to come downstairs to "visit," we would see her sitting upright in it, staring pensively out at the motley crew of pet companions who were beginning to populate my home. By now, I had seven cats who had joined my family.

True to her remote style, she never attacked, nor did she befriend; she just established herself in her own area of the house, and the other cats, even our traumatized cat, Sonny, alias "Sonny Switchblade," gave her wide berth. I believe her invisible cat box boundary was more real than not—it certainly worked for her. To this day, Silk continues to be drawn to boxes, no matter the size, and I often find her sitting in a newly emptied box, looking out with her special brand of quiet dignity.

I made another attempt to find Silk a home. I had a retired couple interested who came over to meet Silk, but while there, they fell in love with another rescue cat I had recently taken in and chose her instead. I can't say that I minded, as I was starting to get attached to Silk and wanted to be sure she found the right match; but personally, I'm almost positive that Silk threw up her invisible-box shield when I set her in the woman's lap. The woman just couldn't "see" her.

By this time, we'd had Silk back in our home for several months, and she was beginning to explore it. She worked her way downstairs via her invisible box, then slipped quietly into the adjacent laundry room, took note of the cat door, analyzed its meaning, and wandered outside. I had hoped she wouldn't discover that because so many adopters need to keep their cats inside, and once a cat discovers the outer world, it's harder for them to be indoor cats. But I didn't have the heart to stop her explorations, so I watched her reenter the world she'd been separated from for over a year. She wandered into it with the quiet fascination and analytical leisure that was so beautiful about her, moving in slow circles further and further from our house with each passing day.

In this way, Silk claimed her summer territory—our small stable. She would return to the house for food, but otherwise I would find her all relaxed and viewing me from the top of a hay bale in the mornings and disappearing to her own outside haunts throughout the days. At this point, I was still determined to find her a home before the winter set in. I was starting to beg people who understood special needs in cat behavior to give her a try, but the conundrum of matching an odd personality cat with a person capable of understanding its quirky behavior is that those people already have too many cats. I wasn't getting any bids anywhere.

Finally, it happened. Silk chose us. That's the best way I can explain it. She'd analyzed the location, the circumstances, and all her probable companions to her complete satisfaction and we were "The One."

Here's how she told me:

One morning, Silk ran past me on the stairwell, and I noticed she had something in her mouth. Upstairs, she started meowing loudly, which is not Silk's style, as she's always been quiet. I followed her upstairs to see what was going on and discovered that she had set down a living baby bunny at the top of the stairs. Oddly, she didn't fight me when I took the rabbit and set it free.

. . . .

The next morning, Silk ran past me again as I was coming downstairs, and I followed her to see that she'd laid a still-living bird down at the top of the stairs. Once again, I took the bird, without her fighting me for it, and set it free.

The third morning, Silk once again ran past me as I was coming downstairs, and this time, she laid a very frightened mole at the top of the stairs. Once again, she did not fight me for rights to the mole, and I set it free.

Then she was done—she has never brought a catch into this house since those three days in a row, and she has been with us now, permanently, for almost two years.

I knew exactly what she was saying: that she'd accepted this household as hers and that these three specialized gifts (no mice involved) were her way of thanking us for taking her in. We were now officially hers, the same as she was ours—cat contract signed, sealed, and delivered. Now, how in the world was I supposed to send her on to another home after that?

When it turned cold this winter, Silk returned to live inside with us and as yet has shown absolutely no interest in going outside even as the weather warms up. I've even shown her how nice it is outside, but she declines. She continues to be remote in general but is starting to seek attention from me (no one else), even though she doesn't want to be picked up or cuddled in any way. I sometimes insist that she accept my mauling embrace, but she escapes me as gently as she can She doesn't want to hurt my feelings, but she prefers a box, thank you.

Right now, Silk is lying on the desk beside me, basking in the sun. She's not looking out the window though; she's leaning toward me. She's been hanging close to me today ever since I started typing her story, and I swear she can tell I'm thinking intensely about her right now. She will usually, when I'm working, settle down, catstyle, directly on top of what I'm doing so that I can't work without paying attention to her first—but not today. Today, she knows I'm busy writing about her and has given me permission to complete her "forever" story.

PINKY

scaredy cat

Pinky came to me in a roundabout way. My daughter visited friends who had recently discovered her in their backyard. They didn't want her, so my daughter took her in. A year later, my daughter returned home for the summer but now had another stray cat along with its litter of six. We found homes for four of the kittens, and when my daughter moved away, she took the mom and the last two of her kittens. Pinky stayed with me—an easy arrangement since at that time (2004) we only had three cats (Io, History, and Bonzi).

Pinky was a pretty tri-colored calico with mascara-lined, intelligent eyes and three dots on her nose. This seemed to parallel the fact that she only had three legs. Her left front leg was missing. I have no clue how this occurred, as that was her state when my daughter picked her up. I'm told that when pregnant cats are nutritionally deficient, their litter can be born with missing appendages, but Pinky had an intensely nervous disposition, which I attribute to her loss of trust when she lost her leg. I envision a cow stepping on her leg when she was a kitten, permanently pinching off the circulation. There happened to be a dairy farm a short distance behind the house where Pinky showed up, so I think that's a feasible history. I can only imagine the pain that she endured at so young an age as her leg atrophied and fell off.

Whatever her past, Pinky gave meaning to the term "scaredy cat." She didn't ask for much, preferring to roam alone outside most of the time. She would hiss at the other cats, so they left her to her own space. She didn't care for people either; if I talked to her and wooed her, and provided, there was no movement anywhere to scare her off, she would hobble over to me occasionally, meowing loudly of her fears. If I picked her up, she would hiss and fuss in abject stress but never turned on me. From the start of living here, Pinky chose me to trust—but that was it.

I figured Pinky would get over her fears in due time, and she has been making progress. It's been almost six years now, and she occasionally slips around the edges of the living room to sit behind me on the couch. That's about as much exposure as she can handle. One sleepless night, just this winter, I happened to be lying on the couch in the dark awaiting the sunrise when she slipped onto my chest and lay there purring for some time. That was a huge leap of faith for her. She hasn't done it since, but then I haven't been up predawn to lie on the couch either.

Respecting her need to be left alone, she and the members of my family managed to share space together; but as time was passing, I was getting more deeply involved in animal rescues, and the number of animals around the house were increasing. This wasn't something Pinky could adapt to. By the summer of 2007, Pinky was so freaked out by our new permanent cat members—Hobbs, Prince, Buddy, Tippy, and Uma—that she started living in the woods behind the house. Unfortunately, Hobbs and the triplets found it great entertainment to stalk Pinky and watch her run. Pinky gives a grand display of hissing, but she isn't a fighter.

That summer, watching this occur, I started a serious search to find her a home. I knew that her best home would be a quiet one where she would be the only pet—a home where she could cautiously study her landscape and cautiously appear, to be met with silence, while she could slowly establish a sense of safety. This plan was good in theory, but where do you find anyone who is willing to take a neurotic, skittish cat into his home to wait patiently for years until she minimizes her fears? Pinky wasn't exactly a starter-cat personality.

So throughout the summer, I watched helplessly as Pinky fled further and further into the woods. I would call to her each day at dusk, and she would meow loudly and fearfully back while slowly, fearfully, hobbling in to eat; but with each passing week, she returned from a greater distance. Finally, she began to disappear for several days at a time. At one point, she disappeared for over a week. This had me really concerned. I was afraid that coyotes, foxes, or bobcats might find her—my dogs keep watch from the porch at night, but she was moving outside of their protective shield.

I paced and searched the woods to no avail. Then one of the other cats disappeared as well. Mister Buddy, the friendliest of the cats, was gone. At this point, I was sure some wildlife was lurking nearby. I was beside myself, looking and calling each day with no response; then, one early morning I was greeted by Buddy, who nonchalantly, with a big meow "hello," appeared from the woods behind the house. Shortly after his appearance, in came Pinky as well. They were both fat and content, as though they had never left. They were also on good terms, if not friends. At the least, Pinky wasn't afraid of Buddy any longer.

I believe that Buddy went into the woods to find Pinky and bring her back. Perhaps he told her he would protect her from the others if she would just return. Buddy was only two years old that summer, but I think he's so massive that the other cats automatically don't challenge him; thus, his temperament has evolved into the direct opposite of Pinky's.

However, I was now feeling desperate about how to protect Pinky. When she returned with Buddy, I set her up in one of the empty dog pens and kept her there for three days. This way, none of the cats could bother Pinky, and she would feel safe while still being outside. Pinky didn't resist this setup in the least; in fact, she appeared very satisfied with it. After three days, I propped the gate just enough for her to go out, and ever since then, from spring to fall, Pinky responds to my evening calls to her by arriving slowly, watchfully, and fretfully voicing her ever-present Pinky fears. Eventually she zips into her pen and, with a look of feline contentment, settles down to eat while I lock her in for the night.

This was a great setup, and I congratulated myself on my creative response to a special needs pet, but when winter arrived, I wasn't sure how to proceed. I started out by insulating her doghouse, placing a front on it with a cat-sized doorway and filling it with straw. I named it "Pinky's Palace" because it was looking so comfy and safe, and Pinky, after a certain amount of anxiety about the changes, accepted this. I suppose she was better off than many pets left outside for the winter, but I wanted to be sure this was her choice. So when the temperature fell below the thirties and Pinky wasn't leaving her house even in the daytime, I tried introducing her to the house. I brought her in and set her down inside the front door, leaving it open so she could make the choice to stay inside or leave. She responded by hobbling rapidly to the living room and tucking herself in behind our TV station.

Since then, she has lived in that corner every winter for the past three years. She has a bed, food, water, and a small litter box all to herself. I installed a pheromone diffuser, which serves to alleviate cat stress, in the outlet over her head, and there she sprawls, regal as a queen, while the cold winds blow outside.

Occasionally, on sunny, calm winter days, she'll let me know—with much noisemaking and changes of mind—that she's ready for a slip outside where she will establish herself on the woodpile preening in the sun. At night, I call her, and she will pop up from under the porch, crying loudly and hysterically while I run across the porch in my bare feet to lift her (hissing but agreeable) and bring her in.

Sometimes, Pinky and I play this "catch-and-mouse" game several times before she allows me to pick her up. Infuriatingly, she will stand at the very edge of the porch as I brace myself against the winds and chill to get to her, and then, at the last second, she will decide she's still too afraid and disappear with a wave of her tail back under the porch.

I have to laugh at the comedy that plays out between us at these times. I return to the house, cussing, to warm up while she makes up her mind that perhaps she is ready to confront the harrowing passage from the porch to behind the TV set; and then she pops up at the end of the porch, and we try again.

Always, when the grand moment arrives, and she *finally* allows me to wrap my hands around her belly, lifting her into the relative safety of my arms, I experience the essential gift bequeathed to me from her. As I watch her scamper off to her hideaway where she will tuck in all warm and safe, I know that I've managed to make something good happen for an animal that otherwise didn't stand a chance. As the saying goes: Saving one pet doesn't change the world, but for that one pet, the world changes forever. Amen.

MURPHY

the gentleman and the gauntlet

The first time I met Murphy, he was a gray blur. This is not an uncommon sight for me. I keep a bowl of dry food in the woodshed for my cat crew, and this sometimes lures in strays who fly by me, fearful of being reproached. Usually this is the only sighting I get of them, but Murphy had a double reason for remaining. At the time, I had a cat I had rescued who was nursing a litter, and thus, not yet fixed. Murphy was not fixed either. They actually made a beautiful, regal couple as, most mornings, I could see them warming themselves together on the picnic table. He with his gray, tiger-swirled coat, white bib, white-booted feet and gray, black, white with slips of cream, marked face; she with her long fur, mascara-marked green eyes, and glinting gold, white, and black markings.

I decided if he was going to hang around the premises, he'd best be wormed; so one morning, I offered him some wet food with wormer in it, and that sealed the deal. No longer was Murphy a blur on the horizon—he just settled right in.

It was obvious that he was designed to be a large cat. His head was immense, perched squarely on a thick, muscular neck, and he had eight toes on each of his front feet, giving him a gigantic, boxing-gloved look; but he was as gentle as a gentleman can be. He would purr contentedly next to anyone who happened to be in the yard and surprise them with a fleet-footed but gentle leap into their lap. His special pleasure was to sit by us at the picnic table to beg for goodies. Well, to be honest, "beg" is something we had to teach him. At first, his motive was to get in close, purring away, then quickly reach out with that massive spoon-sized paw of his and swipe the food right off the plate. Instruction about that kind of behavior had to be given. He finally stopped doing it after he'd put on some weight and knew there would always be enough food, but he still makes himself comfortable near the picnic table when food is being served.

Murphy had an odd glitch though. He was happy as a purring clam when being petted; but if I began to rub his belly, I would find my hand engulfed in all four paws, claws extended and a mouthful of teeth. Not enough to penetrate the skin, but enough to require careful extrication of my hand via some serious maneuvering. I thought this was just a "thing" of his about his belly, but he eventually showed me that it was more than that.

One day, I was working in the garden when he came up to me, pointedly dug a hole, and relieved himself at my feet. Now, as any cat lover knows, cats tend to be private about their doings, but what caught my eye immediately was that his stool was runny and dark colored. I'm quite sure that Murphy orchestrated this intentionally—that he wanted to show me his dilemma. I took this stool sample in to the vet, which checked out to be a severe intestinal infection probably caused by unchecked worm infestation. The vet tech declared that that was the worst case she'd ever seen, so I imagine the poor dude's intestines were pretty tender by the time he found us. Today, he doesn't care if I rub his belly and has also never relieved himself near me since.

I really, truly planned to find Murphy a home. By this summer of 2008, I had nine cats and was astounded that this had happened, though I'm finding that "too many cats" is a common occurrence if one goes deep enough into rescue work. It's like wearing a badge of honor. At some point, either you have bonded so deeply that you can't give the cat up or (more likely) the rescue cat is so neurotic, no one will take it, and it's then yours by default.

In Murphy's case, our reason was the former. We all fell in love with Murphy; he was such a pleasant guy. I did make a weak attempt to advertise for a home and had two responses, but both would have relegated Murphy to an indoor existence, and we just couldn't see the regal, earthy-looking and massive-sized Murphy looking out a window at a world he couldn't access. So we waited for a "better placement" until we were thoroughly hooked. Not just me either, my hubby too—the practical one.

Murph, true to his good looks and manly attitude, seemed to have a thing for the ladies right from the start, and they for him too. I've mentioned Nutmeg, the mother cat, who was eventually homed; then Uma and he "dated" for a while, as Uma loves the classy men. I recently saw him touch noses with Io, which is a small miracle because Io just does not allow anyone anywhere near her without hissing. It took him a while, but even she allows him into her personal space. That's something.

In the time he's been with us, he's shown no interest in using his great size against the others. He will simply sit and look solidly at his aggressors until they realize he isn't going to run or fight; then I've watched him bring his face in really close and touch noses. Competition over.

He had to take a whacking from Sonny though. Sonny wasn't going to let it go with just a big "stupid" face looking back at him—no way. So one day, Murphy showed up with a chunk out of his left ear, and I'm sure it was Sonny "Switchblade's" doing. Murph's wound was sensitive and took a while to heal, and he will now always have a gash there. I felt bad about our problem child being so harsh on the lovable Murph, but I haven't seen Sonny stalking Murph since then so I guess that was their truce.

Heaven forbid, though, that this would be the end of it. Murph had one more gauntlet to run if he was to merge peacefully into my ever-growing menagerie, an unexpected one. Prince took deep, dark, squinty-eyed offense at my husband's growing approval of Murphy.

From a kitten, Prince, our sharp-thinking Siamese mix, always proffered unusual feline loyalty to my husband. He will always run up to greet him when he gets home, and though Prince will accept a petting from most anyone, he will *only* lap-sit with my husband. There he will assume a relaxed and self-assured stance as regal as an Egyptian cat portrait and looking as protective of his human property as a, well, a prince.

However, despite this singularly worshipful stance, he never had a problem with "his human" liking the other cats, until Murphy. The very second my spouse started to bond with Murphy, Prince was enraged. Just like a cat, naturally intuitive, he immediately recognized competition for "his human's" heart and he wasn't going to live with that!

So what does a slight-boned, nonaggressive cat do when he seeks vengeance against a massively built, one-swipe-could-take-you-down competitor? Why, enlist the help of a big brother, of course. We watched, mystified, as Prince enrolled Buddy in a gang-war against Murphy. The two brothers began to co-stalk Murphy throughout the property days on end, while he, in turn, worked just as hard to ignore them and go about his business.

What was hilarious about this setup was that Buddy didn't have a clue about being aggressive; that wasn't his style at all, so there is this big, happy hippo of a cat trying so hard to back his brother when he was actually terror-struck at the idea of being involved in a cat fight! (In truth, Buddy never even caught a mouse or a bird in his entire life.) The offshoot was that Buddy began chewing on my plants and throwing up; the poor guy's belly was in a terrible, nervous uproar!

We finally had to step in and attempt to break up the dead lock—we, as a rule, make it clear that cat fights are unacceptable in our peaceful kingdom, and this is heeded up to a point. (Sonny, to date, is the only one who just can't seem to stop himself when he's in a mood, though he's slowed down.) We made a determined point of officiously scattering the three of them when we saw them in a tight circle doing their so-catlike, calm-before-the-storm stare down. For anyone who doesn't know cat behavior, this silent treatment is intended to build into an explosion of fur-flying frenzy complete with noteworthy sounds of hissing and yowling.

After a couple weeks of us stalking them stalking Murphy, they stopped stalking Murphy. Personally, I believe both Buddy and Prince were relieved that they had an excuse to end the war.

Lately, it's been peaceful around here, and just this morning, I watched as Murphy and Prince walked past each other—almost touching—in order to get to some tuna treats I was setting out. *They completely ignored each other!*

So I believe it's almost over, but there are new rules in place. As long as my husband behaves himself by ignoring Murphy (in Prince's presence) and Murphy never ever comes upstairs (which is *absolutely* Prince's domain), I believe we can all live happily ever after, enclosed within the watchtowers of the kingdom of Prince—and Murph's okay with that too.

• • • • • • •

LOKI

lil' stretch man

Loki came to me as a three-month-old kitten in August of 2008. We had ten cats by this time, and I had absolutely no intentions of keeping another, especially a kitten that could more easily be homed. With my ten, the seams of this homestead were stretched to maximum capacity.

My neighbors, who turned him over to me, said that they had interceded when they heard the owners were going to drop him off at a shelter where they knew he would be put down. He was a sickly kitten, with eye discharge, a runny nose, and an ongoing sneeze. His ears were so full of dark gunk that I had to help the vet hold him down while she dug into his ears to clean them. The antibiotics for his sneeze were ineffective after two series, and the vet said this might be due to nutritional deficiencies.

"He may always be a sneezer," she told me. (It took a year, but he's not sneezing anymore.) He tested negative for disease so, gratefully, the sneezing wasn't indicative of serious health problems.

Loki was an orange and white tabby cat with unusual eyes that seemed to melt into you. His eyes were his main feature of connection to us at the time because his personality was kept well under wraps. He didn't seem to care much for humans and didn't seek our attention. I surmise that he never had much human interaction—just enough to keep him from being completely feral. I knew this apathy toward people would not show well at the vet's office where I'd planned to display him, so I decided to hold onto him and search for a home that would be compatible with his evasive personality.

Time passed without any adoptive home appearing, and Loki slowly worked his way out of the bedroom where he stayed, then downstairs, past my cats who barely took note of his presence and eventually found his way to the outside cat door. I never point out the cat door to my foster kittens; but given enough time here, they have all found it. It's magical when they do as they open their eyes upon a whole new and brilliant world to explore. I can almost see the light of curious pleasure spread across their features when they first slip outside. It's a very special moment, and I'm always delighted if I'm around to notice it when it happens.

After watching Loki experience that moment, I would catch sight of him here and there outside. One day, he discovered our front porch. Eureka! I think the little lad was beside himself with ecstasy. For weeks after this discovery, I saw little of him other than when he would suddenly zip out and then zip back under the porch as though savoring the reality of an under-porch. He became so obviously connected to the porch as his place to be that I concluded this had been his original "home"— Loki had been born under someone's porch.

Now that he had chosen to live outside, Loki began to befriend my male cats, or perhaps my male cats began to befriend him. Sonny Sunshine, showing us he actually had a soft spot in his nugget of a heart, would stalk Loki and gently wrestle with him in the yard. Some time later, early one morning, I caught Mr. Hobbs holding Loki down in a full-bodied lockdown while washing his head and face. Hobbs has always been secretive about his doings, but I've caught him wrestling and cleaning Loki often since then. Eventually, as Loki got over his fixation of living under the porch, he began to share the second floor of the woodshed with Hobbs. I took that to indicate that they had agreed to be full-fledged, semi-feral brothers.

I also noticed that Prince, Buddy, and Murphy would nod at him as they walked by, and my female felines, every one, just chose to ignore him. Loki passed the cat community acceptance exam with not a flinch. Impressive.

• • • • • • • •

Meanwhile, Loki found himself a new obsession: birds.

As summer turned into fall, I hung the birdfeeder from a tree limb for the winter. Loki began to study the birdfeeder. He spent days and days, which turned into weeks and weeks, staring at the feeder from below. Finally, he climbed up the tree and sat directly over it. He tried reaching down to get the pretty birdies, but that wasn't going to work. I watched him trying and trying to get at those birds and shook my head and laughed at his grim determination. We have set up our birdfeeder to be cat proof.

Nonetheless, Loki was absolutely obsessed. Immediately after breakfast each morning from fall through the winter (such was his obsession), out went Loki to the birdfeeder. Cold, wet, windy, or snow-covered, the little Loki could be seen studying that birdfeeder. He was either sitting beneath it or sitting over it throughout each and every day, only staying in when the temperatures were frostbitingly frigid.

Spring of 2009 came, and Loki was still hard at it; I was still giggling at his impossible obsession when one morning, I glimpsed an orange streak flying up through the air, and to my horror, Loki landed with a bird in his mouth. I think he was as surprised as I was that his technique had worked, and when I chased him down, Loki dropped the bird, and it flew off. So I moved the feeder up even higher, but it took no time at all before Loki used his exceptionally long body to jettison himself straight up into the air and grab another bird right off the feeder! Back to the cat-resistant bird feeder drawing board I went. I finally dug out some tightly knit cage wire we had and wrapped it all around the bird feeder. This made an ugly mess of wire and twine hanging from the tree, and the birds took a while figuring out how to land inside it; but Loki couldn't score. Shortly after that, he appeared to lose interest. I hope so because, as you know, Loki had become a keeper.

I couldn't tell you when precisely he transformed from "rescued stray" into a "member of the family." Perhaps it was when I saw Sonny and Hobbs, our hardcore bachelors, adopting him; perhaps when he fell so in love with the underside of our porch that my motherly heart when out to him; or maybe when we realized he didn't ask for much from any of us. It was a slow, quiet, undercurrent through which he moved into our hearts.

Paradoxically, occasionally, and without notice, he chooses to sleep with us at night, and you'd never know at those times that he is as aloof as he tends to be. During these inexplicable moods, he insists on sleeping near my head, and preferably, if he can, on top of my chest (directly over my heart), while emitting this soft, tender, cat purr and looking directly into my eyes, bespeaking deep feline gratitude. He is a sensitive guy.

Most likely, Loki slipped impenetrably into my heart when early in the spring, I briefly fostered a stray dog. New dogs within the household affect my cat population in various ways. Some of my cats just tell the dog to shove over in no uncertain terms, some run when the dog comes out to "play," and some disappear from sight until the dog leaves. Loki, along with Hobbs and Buddy, disappeared. Shortly after I'd placed the dog, Buddy appeared, then a day or so later, Hobbs surfaced, but no Loki. Several more days passed and still no Loki. This worried me. Loki is a prowler. His territory extends past the safe parameters that the rest of my cats stay within. We are surrounded by woods and fields, and anything's possible past the protected areas so well-guarded by my dogs. Could he have wandered too far this time? Could he be lost or hurt or dead?

So in desperation after a week of watching for his return, with no other option to finding him, I decided to meditate on Loki. Around 7:00 a.m., I emptied my mind, tuned into him, and visualized Loki held securely in my arms. I called to him from my heart to come home and told him that he was now safe.

That day, 10:00 a.m., Loki appeared.

Since then, Loki has been getting friendlier with us. He continues to entertain himself outside most of the time but has been sleeping on the topside of the porch during the day; lately, I've seen him settled in for the night on the porch as well. He's much more likely to allow himself to be seen, and more and more often, will curl himself next to me for a prolonged nap and cuddle. Right now, as I type this, he's here stretched out on the floor at my feet. He came upstairs to find me and made me stop writing to visit with me a bit. This is not the norm for Loki, but I'm beginning to understand the concept of cats having nine lives. Watching emotionally wounded pets shift from personalities engendering fear or anger or remoteness to trust and love and companionship is one of the richest rewards inherent to rescue work. Given the simple ingredients of the time and space they need, combined with a caretaker's patience, understanding, and attention, they heal, and they change.

As I pause to return Loki's bid for attention, I can see that Loki's second life is now emerging—and it's going to be so much better than his first.

Clockwise from top:
Buddy, Silk, and Io

Top: Prince and Uma. Bottom: Pinky's Palace.

Clockwise from top left: Uma on the night she came home, a year later, and on her perch

Top: Prince. Bottom: Loki.

Clockwise from top: The bros: Prince and Buddy, Murphy and Hobbs, and Silk.

Top: Mister Hobbs. Bottom: Tippy.

Top: Murphy displays his eight-toed paws. Bottom: Mister Hobbs.

Top: Silk using the back window exit. Bottom: Sonny Sunshine.